Grapes

Morris L. Venden

PACIFIC PRESS PUBLISHING ASSOCIATION
Boise, Idaho
Oshawa, Ontario, Canada

Designed by Tim Larson
Cover illustration by Nery Cruz

Library of Congress Cataloging in Publication Data

Venden, Morris L.
  Grapes.

  1. Bible. N.T. John XV, 1-8—Meditations. I. Title.
BS2615.4.V46   1986   226'.506   85-17296

ISBN 0-8163-0623-0

87 88 89 90 91 ● 6 5 4 3 2

Contents

Introduction

A grapevine bears grapes because it is a grapevine, never in order to be one. The branches on the grapevine bear grapes because they are connected to the grapevine, never in order to become connected.

Jesus used the analogy of the vineyard to teach some vital spiritual lessons. Jesus was the greatest Teacher the world has ever known. The simplicity of His teaching and His methods needs to be copied today. Christ preached to the common people. He came to preach the gospel to the poor. He reached people where they were and brought plain, simple truth to their comprehension. No one needed to go to a dictionary to obtain the meaning of His words. He presented truth to the minds of the people in forceful yet simple language. No one needed to consult the learned doctors as to His meaning. As when we go to John 15 to study Jesus' teaching about the vineyard, we experience the simplicity of the greatest Teacher.

Today there is a great deal of dialogue and discussion concerning theological issues. Many people are uneasy and restive and confused. We need to wander around in the vineyard with Jesus, listen to His simple teachings, and be spiritually refreshed.

"I am the true vine,
and my Father is the husbandman." John 15:1.

The True Vine

Have you ever looked closely at a grapevine? I don't mean during the summertime when the branches are in foliage. I mean during the winter, when you can see the vine itself. Do you think it's beautiful? Why, it's ugly, isn't it? When there are no leaves on the branches, you can see the bare vine, black and knotted and gnarled and crooked, looking as though it will never live again.

It reminds us of the One of whom it was said that He was a root out of dry ground. Some of the medieval drawings and carvings of Christ depict Him as rather plain and unattractive. Some of us respond unfavorably to that. But let's not forget that Jesus' beauty was internal, rather than external. Isaiah 53:2 says that "when we shall see him, there is no beauty that we should desire him."

"Only a mother could love this person!" Perhaps you have met someone who impressed you this way on first aquaintance. But as you came to know that person you discovered to your surprise that he or she was a truly beautiful person. Have you ever had this happen?

So when we think of the Vine and when we focus our attention on Him, we are not thinking of someone with external beauty. We are thinking of One whose beauty came from within and from His connection with heavenly sources.

In Old Testament analogy, Israel was the vine, but they proved to be an unfruitful vine, and so there is a new application, a new interpretation of the vine through Jesus' words in this chapter.

The children of Israel were supposed to have been God's people, but one of their problems was that individuals thought they were secure solely because of their connection with Israel. The modern application would be those who think of the vine as the church and who think that all we have to do to have certainty of eternal life is to be enrolled in the church books or connect with the church. This is why Jesus' words are particularly applicable when He says, "I am the true vine." John 15:1. Take your attention away from the church for the true meaning of this parable and fasten it solidly on the *true* Vine, Jesus Christ.

There's something else interesting about Jesus' choice of the vineyard to portray Himself and His relationship to His people. A vine is a dependent plant. It does not stand alone, without support. The branches must depend on the vine, it is true. But the vine depends upon other support as well. Jesus came to show us how to depend upon another. As He depended upon His Father, so we are to depend upon Him.

A vine doesn't receive much glory, credit, and honor. When the vine itself is visible, it's not that attractive. But it provides the connection to the source of nourishment for the branches, and it's amazing to discover that the branches, with all their green leaves in the spring and summertime, and their bright colors in the fall, appear more beautiful than the vine.

The vine is simply another symbol of the One who made Himself of no reputation, who took upon Himself the form of a servant, and who was willing to minister to others rather than to draw attention to Himself.

*"I am the true vine,
and my Father is the husbandman." John 15:1.*

The Husbandman

God must love gardens! When He created our world, He placed Adam and Eve in a garden. Even after sin entered and the ground brought forth thorns and thistles, man's assignment was still in a garden. Apparently this was the most effective way for God to reach fallen mankind.

Throughout the Old Testament, the focus on the garden continues. The righteous are called "trees of righteousness, the planting of the Lord." Isaiah 61:3. The godly are likened to trees "planted by rivers of water," that bring forth their fruit in their season. See Psalm 1:3. Israel, as we have already noticed, was compared to a vine. God, as our Shepherd, promises to lead His children in green pastures and beside still waters. See Psalm 23. As prophesied, Jesus came to earth to "grow up . . . as a tender plant." Isaiah 53:2. The promise of the new earth as the future home of God's children is presented by Isaiah as a place where "they shall plant vineyards, and eat the fruit of them." Isaiah 65:21.

Jesus came to show us what God the Father is like, always has been like, and always will be like. So often He compared the Father to a Gardener. In the parable of the barren fig tree, He is the one who planted the tree in His vineyard. See Luke 13. In Matthew 21:33, the Father is the One who "planted a vineyard, and hedged it round about, and digged a winepress in it, and built a tower, and let it out to husbandmen, and went into a far country." In Matthew 20, the Father hired the laborers for a penny a day to work in the fields.

There must be something of particular significance that we can learn about our heavenly Father by comparing Him to a Gardener. Jesus' frequent use of the garden analogy shows its importance in understanding God.

What is a gardener's work? How does a gardener relate to the plants under his care? What methods does a gardener use to bring about favorable results in growing fruit? The patience, the persistence, the continual watchcare, the longing for the harvest—all of these must be pictures of what God is like and how He relates to His children. Watch for Him in this parable of the vineyard of John 15, for God is the Gardener.

"I am the vine,
ye are the branches." John 15:5.

The Branches

Jesus and His disciples were on their way to the Garden of Gethsemane. They had just concluded the time together in the upper room, had just shared the bread and the wine in the Last Supper. There Jesus had washed the disciples' feet, bringing all except one of them to surrender and communion with Him. That one, Judas, had gone forth from the supper to find his way to the high priest and make the final arrangements for betraying his Lord.

As they slowly made their way toward the garden, Jesus and His disciples passed a vineyard, easily identifiable in the bright moonlight. In this final analogy before His crucifixion, Jesus tried once more to show His disciples the relationship they were to sustain with Him, their part in living the life of faith that He had been trying so hard to teach them those past three and a half years.

Jesus said to them, "I am the vine, ye are the branches." Verse 5.

What do branches do?

Well, a branch does one of two things. Either a branch abides and, as a result, brings forth fruit; or a branch does not abide and, as a result, withers, is cast forth as a branch, and cast into the fire and burned. It is either one or the other.

The parable of John 15 is primarily intended for the

branches—not for the vine. In fact, it was given by the Vine to the branches! So it follows then that if we are the branches, this parable is directed to us. If directed at us, then we should look very closely at its meaning.

"Every branch in me that beareth not fruit he taketh away: and every branch that beareth fruit, he purgeth it, that it may bring forth more fruit." John 15:2.

Two Kinds of Branches

Notice that there are two kinds of branches in this parable. One kind of branch does not bear fruit. Does this mean it is possible to have a branch "in Him" that doesn't bear fruit? That's what the text says. It doesn't say "every branch that pretends to be a branch"; it doesn't say "every branch that is only connected to the church." It says "every branch in me."

It must be possible to be in Him and still not bear fruit, at least for a short while. Perhaps Judas was an example of this. Through the power of Christ, he was enabled to raise the dead and heal the sick and cast out devils. Judas was in relationship with Christ for a time, but he did not bear fruit and was taken away. (Please notice who took him away—it was Judas himself! The being taken away was his own personal choice, not some arbitrary act on the part of God.)

It is possible for a person to become a Christian, experience a genuine conversion, and be in the Vine, in Christ, but not stay with that initial breakthrough, not continue that relationship, not go on to absolute surrender—and to bear no fruit and be taken away.

I believe that there are many people who have been converted and who have later apostatized—not because they were never converted, but because they failed to catch the message of this parable. They failed to abide in Christ. This parable

13

deals with the question of once saved, always saved. In simple words, it is possible to be a branch and to leave, to separate oneself from the source of spiritual nourishment.

The second kind of branch is that which bears fruit. It continues to abide in the vine, and the fruit comes as a result. John 15:2 describes this kind of branch by saying, "Every branch that beareth fruit, he purgeth it, that it may bring forth more fruit." We'll look at the purging process in more detail later. But the branch brings forth fruit.

Are you interested in growing grapes? Do you desire the fruits of the Spirit to be seen in your life? Then this parable is for you. It is a parable for the branches that bear fruit.

*"Now ye are clean
through the word which I have
spoken unto you." John 15:3.*

Now Ye Are Clean

What does it mean to become a branch? Well, this parable was given to disciples who had already made the beginning in their Christian life. God has left it to us to decide whether or not we would like to become a branch connected with the Vine.

There's an interesting phrase in verse 16 , where Jesus says, "Ye have not chosen me, but I have chosen you, and ordained you, that ye should go and bring forth fruit." The primary application of this is to the disciples, whom He had chosen as apostles for a special mission in the early church. The Scripture says that He even chose Judas (see John 6:70), although Judas pressed himself into the group of disciples. God is always the initiator in the great plan of salvation.

The lost sheep doesn't seek the shepherd. The fish in the sea don't come to the shore to be caught. The shepherd goes out seeking, and the fisherman goes out fishing. We are all chosen by God, at His initiative. How we respond to His choosing is where our choice comes in.

Let's never forget that every one of us is destined to be saved, eternally saved, unless we resist and turn down God's offer. The people who lose out will have gone to a great deal of trouble to do so, kicking and screaming and fussing all the way! So God has chosen us, and I'm thankful for that today. Aren't you glad of the fact that the great Gardener has chosen every one of us for salvation? That's part of the good news of the gospel.

Well then, what happens when we respond to His choosing? Here are these dry, withered, "wild" branches, as Paul calls them in Romans 11:17, that are somehow grafted into the vine. Of course, the analogy in Romans 11 is the olive tree—so in this mixing of metaphors, we are going to have the branch from a wild olive tree being grafted into a grapevine! At first glance it looks impossible. But as Paul says in Romans 11:24, this grafting is contrary to nature, so we don't have to try to make the analogy stand on all fours. It's contrary to nature, and that's one of the miracles of the plan of salvation.

What are these wild olive branches? They are the souls, dead in trespasses and sins. That's what we are, and we receive life through connection with Christ. It is by faith in Him as our personal Saviour that this union between branch and vine is begun. Do I realize my need of a Saviour? Have I accepted Christ personally? If so, then I am in the vine.

This initial connection with the vine corresponds to what theologians call justification. It is the time when we stand before God as though we had never even sinned. The disciples, to whom Jesus addressed this parable, were in this position. How do we know? We know because of John 15:3: "Now ye are clean through the word which I have spoken unto you."

Just a short time before, these disciples had been bickering and arguing—unwilling to humble themselves and wash one another's feet. But in ministering to them Jesus humbled Himself, and their hearts had been touched. Now He could say to them, Ye are clean. They didn't have a very good track record, yet they didn't have to put in several weeks of good behavior before they could be forgiven. He said, Now ye are clean. Don't you like the sound of those words? We are cleansed as soon as we come to Him.

Not only that, but these disciples were not yet perfect and mature, never to sin or fall or fail again. In just a few hours they forsook Jesus and fled. One of them denied Him. All of them were ashamed of their connection with Him. Their faith failed so miserably in the difficult time of trial.

But Jesus, even though He knew what was going to happen, even though He warned them of what was going to happen, still could say to them, "Now ye are clean." They could be accepted by Him and be branches in the Vine. They didn't have to bring forth the fruit first—but rather, through the continued connection with Him, the fruit resulted.

So this parable in John 15 is primarily for those who have made the beginning in the Christian life. It is a parable for the growing branch, the growing Christian, the one who is seeking to bring forth fruit today.

"Abide in me, and I in you." John 15:4.

Abiding

Reading John 15, you very soon realize that the word *abide* is a key word. What does it mean "to abide"? If you look in the exhaustive concordance, to find every time the word *abide* shows up in Scripture, you will discover that the word *abide* means nothing more than "to stay." The assumption of this parable of the vine and the branches is that if we are invited to stay, we must have already arrived, already come in the first place. It is pointless to urge someone to stay if he has not yet come. There is not much in John 15 on the subject of coming to Christ in the first place. The emphasis is on staying with Him. There's something just as important as getting married—it is staying married. There is something just as important as coming to Christ initially—it is staying with Him. This is Jesus' burden in His words recorded in John 15. Here we see an indication of how our power of choice is to operate in the Christian life.

I am going to take the position, on the basis of case histories and surveys, that most people who have joined the church and have known something of the wonders of redeeming grace, have not stayed there. Most of them have allowed the enemy to snatch them away, by degrees—slowly and imperceptibly—to snatch them away from the realization and excitement of God's grace. They have come to substitute, in place of abiding in the

Vine, simply abiding in the vineyard (the church) or abiding in other branches (other people).

We have noticed that in John 15 Jesus was not speaking of abiding in the church. It isn't enough to abide in the company of other believers, and yet that's one of our traps. We can be outwardly united to Christ, and yet there may be no vital connection to the vine. Then there will be no growth or fruitfulness. There may be an apparent connection to Christ, a profession of religion, but no real union with God by faith. Those who bear no fruit to God's glory are false branches and show that they have not been abiding in the vine.

Perhaps the closest most of us come to the grafting process is to transplant something into our gardens. Have you ever done it? It is possible to transplant several similar-looking plants into the same plot of ground, using the same technique, so far as it is possible to measure. Some of the plants will flourish, and some will die. At the time of transplanting, everything looks the same. Apparently the plants have all taken root in their new environment. But let a little time go by, a few showers, a few days of sunshine, and it becomes very obvious which plants are going to live and which ones will not. What makes the difference? One is connected to the soil; the other is not.

So how do you abide in the vine? How do you maintain this connection with Christ? Have you come to the end of your own resources, not only once, but on a daily basis? A plant in the garden that has been transplanted can last for a short time on its own resources. But unless it taps the nourishment available in the soil, its own resources will give out, and it will wither and decay. Is your communion with God top priority with you, or are you still merely trying to *do* the things that please God?

Let's notice the deeper meaning of abiding. "Abide in me, and I in you." What does it mean for Christ to be in you, or for you to be in Christ? Obviously it is referring to a very close relationship. That's what it means. Christ is saying, "Stay in the relationship you began when you first accepted Me as your only hope. Stay in relationship with Me."

It is possible, in fact usual, for a servant/master relationship to not be close; in fact, it may be quite distant. It is possible to have an employer/employee relationship that is far from mutual respect. It is possible to have a teacher/student relationship that is very casual. You ideally have a truly *intimate* relationship with one special person in your life. That's where Jesus' analogy of marriage and His church comes in. When we talk about an abiding relationship in the setting of this parable, we are talking about an intimate, loving relationship. There is no such thing as an intimate, loving relationship without fellowship and communication. Jesus is saying, "Please, I want to know you. I want you not only to begin with Me, but to stay with Me. Are you interested?"

"Oh," someone says, "That's a works trip. To emphasize the continuing relationship with Christ is simply legalism." Yes, for anyone who hasn't come to the end of his own resources yet, anything, including this, can be a works trip. The person who is still depending upon his connection to the vineyard or to the other branches (even to the branch occupying the pulpit—and please don't make that mistake!) is going to find emphasis upon abiding in the vine a works trip. That's true. But once a person has seen the love and kindness of Jesus, as demonstrated by His life and death, and has caught a glimpse of His care for each of us, he's going to look at abiding as a great privilege and high honor. To him, Bible study and prayer is no longer a bore, but a fantastic opportunity.

Back to your own garden—do you consider it a works trip to leave rosebushes in the ground, where they can partake of the nutrients found in the soil? Imagine a gardener who would say, "Leaving a plant in the dirt is a works trip. I'll put mine there someday, when I feel like it. But I'm not going to be tied to some routine. Some days I'll take my rosebush and carry it with me all through the day. Some days I'll put my rosebush on the bookshelf and let it sit. Some days I'll leave my rosebush lying in the grass, with its roots exposed. And then, when I feel the need, I'll stick it back into its hole in the ground." How many roses would bloom under such conditions?

Please notice that when Jesus uses the word *abide* in His instructions to His disciples in this parable, He is indicating where our effort and our choice really lie. I had a student come and tell me that he was very discouraged and frustrated because of the complexities of living the Christian life. He said that he just couldn't get it all together. But *we* don't have to get it all together! The truth is that the human effort and willpower and the direction of our choice in living the Christian life is just this simple. "Stay with Me," said Jesus, "in abiding, continuing fellowship." That's it.

How is that accomplished? Please don't fall into the trap of thinking that we stay in relationship with someone by trying to do things to please them. That is not the way we stay in relationship with anybody. Colossians 2:6 gives us a clue: "As ye have therefore received Christ Jesus the Lord, so walk ye in him." We walk with Him, we fellowship with Him, we stay with Him, in the same way that we received Him at first. How did we receive Him at first? "By the deeds of the law there shall no flesh be justified in his sight: for by the law is the knowledge of sin." Romans 3:20. So we did not receive Christ at first through the deeds of the law. "Now to him that worketh is the reward not reckoned of grace, but of debt. But to him that worketh not, but believeth on him that justifieth the ungodly, *his faith is counted for righteousness.*" Romans 4:4, 5, emphasis supplied.

We accepted Jesus in the first place and became attached to the Vine, not by trying to produce good deeds that would make us worthy, but by accepting His grace as a mighty gift. Now let's not imply that accepting His grace has no work attached to it. Most sinners have discovered that it is hard work to come to Christ. However, it is a different type of work from the deeds work that Paul is talking about. Paul is not campaigning for an effortless, do-nothing religion. He is reminding us of the real effort involved. The work, if we want to call it work, is in admitting that we can do nothing and in coming to Him to accept His grace.

In John 15 Jesus tells us where the effort should be directed. He never asks us to work on producing fruit—He tells us to abide in Him. And if we choose to abide in Him, the fruit is a natural and spontaneous result of that abiding.

So this parable settles the questions of where you place your effort. Yet most of us have had a long pilgrimage of doing everything else but abiding in this close, intimate, loving relationship.

To those of us who have been working on everything else, Christ again today extends His loving invitation, "Abide in me, and I in you."

*"As the branch cannot
bear fruit of itself, except it
abide in the vine; no more can ye,
except ye abide in me." John 15:4.*

Abide in the Vine

My wife and I brought home a particular plant from the nursery one day. It was doing quite well in the bucket, and it was awhile before we got around to transplanting it. But finally it began to outgrow the bucket, and so I picked a spot at random, without my wife's counsel, and put the plant there.

As a result of my planting it in the wrong place, I had to dig it up and transplant it again. But *I* didn't like the looks of it in that spot, so I dug it up and transplanted it once again. The plant is getting a little tired! About the time it's little roots began to get enmeshed and fused with the soil, along comes this gardener and digs it up again. The last I looked, it wasn't doing too well, and its leaves were drooping.

As we study this parable of the vineyard, we come to the realization that it is not an on-again, off-again connection that enables the vine to bear fruit. Even when the branch stays connected to the vine, there is still a growth process going on.

This becomes very intriguing, because I think most of us are aware that even though we have chosen to stay with Christ, our immaturity is often demonstrated, and we are painfully aware that the job is not yet complete. Are you aware of that in your own experience?

We accepted Jesus in the first place by faith in Him as our personal Saviour. That's how the union with the vine is formed.

That is also how it is continued. We accepted Jesus in the first place only after recognizing the love of God and the truth of the gospel. And that is how the abiding is maintained, not only at the beginning of the Christian life, but as a continuation of it. The just shall *live* by faith. We become justified in the first place by accepting of His grace; we continue with Him by faith, and by faith alone. See Hebrews 10:38; Habakkuk 2:4; Romans 1:17. The just have always lived by faith. It isn't by faith plus or minus anything else, it is by faith alone.

It is of utmost importance to realize that Jesus is not placing the responsibility of our works, or our fruit bearing, upon us. It is true that we are to bear fruit, but this is accomplished by faith alone. The branch cannot bear fruit of itself, except it abide in the vine. But if it abide in the vine, it will bring forth much fruit. The fruit is the natural result of abiding in Christ.

Some of us have gotten terribly excited with this realization that the gospel, and how it works in the ongoing Christian life, is just that simple. It is so simple that the boys and girls can understand it, and that is good news indeed. For too long many of us have had the idea that we were to do some part of the work alone. We trusted in Christ for the forgiveness of sin, but then we sought by our own efforts to live for Him. It's a dead-end street. Every failure on the part of God's people is due, not to their lack of trying hard to produce fruit, but due to their lack of faith and trust in Him. And it is by hearing the word of God and communing with Him that faith comes.

We are reminded of the man, in the olden days, walking along the road with a pack on his back. Another man comes by with a horse and buggy. The horse looks a little tired, and the buggy looks a little small, and when the man with the pack on his back is invited aboard for a ride, he leaves the pack on his back, because he doesn't think it would be fair to make the driver and his horse carry the pack too.

Another man boards a boat on the Mississippi River. He has a ticket for a four-day journey, but he's brought along crackers and cheese to eat, because he can't afford to buy food aboard the ship. Every meal, while the rest of the people go to eat, he hides behind a smokestack and eats his crackers and cheese, until they become moldy and he feels about ready to starve. Then they discover him there, and say, "What's the matter with you, man? When you bought your ticket, you also paid for all your meals. Come on and eat with the rest of us."

We accept God's grace, and we say, That's marvelous. He's made provision to save me eternally in heaven. Now I must carry my own pack, and we are bowed beneath the labor. He has invited us to the marriage supper of the Lamb, for fellowship with Him, and we think we have to bring our own food. We accept His mighty gospel as a gift and are thrilled with it, but the thrill dies out, because we fail to see that in walking and fellowshipping with Him, we work by the same method, the same process. We keep wanting to add something to it, and so it becomes a painful process for us not only to come to Him, but also to let Him take our burdens, our sins, our failures, and give us the power for obedience we so sadly lack. We don't fully realize the exciting fact that He wants to give us obedience and victory as gifts.

Abiding in the vine does not take place automatically. Jesus gives it as a plea, an entreaty, a command, if you please, "Abide in Me." Separated from the vine, the branch cannot live. No more, says Jesus, can you live apart from Me. It is only through continual communion with Him that we will grow. No branch will produce fruit if it is only occasionally connected to the vine. The connection must be consistent. The branch must *abide* in the vine.

We are talking about communion with Christ, every day, every hour. It is our privilege to have communion with Christ as a way of life. How much time have you spent in communion with God this past week? Does abiding in Christ sound intangible to you? It's the same vital union that is represented in John 6 by eating His flesh and drinking His blood. John 6:63 gives a clue: "The words that I speak unto you, they are spirit, and they are life." So it is through the Bible and through prayer that we abide in Him, and if we do not abide in Him, we bear no fruit and are taken away.

Continual communion does not insist on continual talking. To pray without ceasing means unbroken union with God. Have you ever traveled with your family for miles without saying a word? And yet you experienced companionship and communion. Our best friends are the ones with whom we are relaxed enough so that we don't have to be having words go on all the time. That is the kind of communion we can have with Jesus, our best Friend. There will be times when we will be communicating directly, and other times when we will just enjoy the privilege of being together, working together, traveling together.

To communicate with the King of the universe should be counted a great privilege, shouldn't it? I see two men, going along the trail toward Emmaus. A Stranger joins them. Their hearts burn within them. But it's getting late when they arrive at home, so they say to the Stranger, "Stay with us, abide with us." They responded to Jesus even though they didn't know who the Stranger was. See Luke 24.

My friend, it's getting late today. The signs all foretell that it's getting late. It's getting dark out there. Won't you join these two disciples who responded, and as you listen to Jesus' invitation, "Abide with Me," why not join them and say, "Come and abide with us." He always does, He always will, because He wants to be with us now and forever.

"I am the vine, ye are the branches: He that abideth in me, and I in him, the same bringeth forth much fruit." John 15:5.

Much Fruit

Fruit is one of the most spontaneous things that happens with a true vine and branches. If you want grapes, you don't work at producing the grapes. Some people have tried. They have produced plastic grapes. One time I bit down on one, by mistake, and it was very disappointing. They may look good on the outside, but that's as far as it goes. No one can produce a genuine grape apart from the product of the vine.

What do the grapes represent? "Being filled with the fruits of righteousness, which are by Jesus Christ, unto the glory and praise of God." Philippians 1:11. Please notice that first of all, the fruits are fruits of righteousness, and second, the fruits are unto the praise and glory of God. And, of course, Galatians 5:22, 23 speaks of the fruits of the Spirit, love, joy, peace, long-suffering, and so forth.

So the grapes are the fruit of righteousness, and righteousness is spontaneous for the branch that is connected to the true Vine.

This brings us to the basic premise of the parable of the vineyard. A grapevine bears grapes because it is a grapevine, never in order to be one. "The Saviour does not bid the disciples labor to bear fruit. He tells them to abide in Him."—*The Desire of Ages,* p. 677. So the effort in the Christian life is always toward the abiding, never toward the fruit. It is toward fellowship with

29

Jesus, toward staying in the Vine, never toward producing righteousness. It is in staying connected with Jesus, never toward trying to be good. This is one of the simple, timeless truths that are taught by the simple analogy of the vine and the branches, Jesus' own statement on the subject.

Sometimes people are afraid that if we concentrate on putting our effort toward the day-by-day relationship and abiding in Christ, that we are somehow against fruit, or antagonistic to it. They fear that the result of not laboring to bear fruit will result in no fruit. But this is not the case. What does Jesus say the result will be? The result will be *"much* fruit."

Are you interested in "much fruit"? Then turn your attention away from the fruit and concentrate on abiding in the vine. It is the only method for producing genuine fruit, genuine righteousness, genuine obedience unto the glory and praise of God.

Plastic grapes? Those don't bring glory to God. They bring glory to the person. A Laodicean church is rich in plastic grapes, but bankrupt of righteousness. Plastic grapes are the worst kind of grapes.

No grapes at all? Well, according to Revelation 3:15, that's getting closer! Isn't that what it says? "I would thou wert cold or hot." God apparently sees greater potential in no grapes at all, than He sees in the plastic grapes of self-righteousness.

But through connection with the Vine, through communion with Him, through abiding in Him we are enabled to bring forth the real thing. We will then know the secret to bearing fruit, genuine fruit, much fruit. Since this is accomplished only by God working in us, "to will and to do of his good pleasure" (see Philippians 2:13), He is the One who gets the credit for it. The glory and praise go to Him.

*"I am the vine, ye are
the branches: He that abideth in
me, and I in him, the same bringeth
forth much fruit: for without me
ye can do nothing." John 15:5.*

Ye Can Do Nothing

Some people are afraid of a do-nothing religion. This verse in John 15 almost sounds like it. "Without me ye can do nothing." The verse begins with one of the "I am" statements of Jesus. It's interesting to trace those particular statements through the gospels. They indicate that Jesus was more than mere man. If anyone else were to say, "Without me ye can do nothing," it would be the height of arrogance. To be able to make such a statement indicates that Jesus was more than mere man. We know, if we have studied His words at all, that although Jesus lived as man, He talked as God. This is one of those occasions.

These words are straight from Jesus' own lips, the kind that would be printed in red in a red-letter edition. Notice His words, "*I am* the vine, ye are the branches." *I* am the Vine. You are *not* the vine. You are the branches. And "without me ye can do nothing."

Let's keep in mind that Jesus addressed these words to His disciples, twelve minus one, for they had just left the upper room on their way to Gethsemane. He is talking about the kind of fruit that is produced in the growing Christian life. He is not talking about the kind of fruit produced by a person who can make a million by his own ingenuity. He is not talking about the one who can get his name in lights or in the headlines, so long as God keeps his heart beating. Jesus is not talking here to skeptics and infidels and atheists. His primary thrust is to the church, to the disciples, to the followers of Jesus. This has a heavy bearing on what we consider in terms of fruit. As we have already noticed, this is the fruit of righteousness.

With these things in mind, let's notice several major points concerning this verse. First of all, when Jesus says, "Without me ye can do nothing," although it's stated negatively, it is also positive. For with Him we can do all things. See Philippians 4:13. Therefore, there is hope for doing.

As wonderful as salvation is and as certain as our assurance of eternal life, there is also hope that, for those who submit to Him, Jesus can fulfill His purpose of living His life in them and bringing forth much fruit. There is hope for a harvest, for produce, for results here and now in the Lord's vineyard. God Himself is interested in fruit. God Himself is anxious to see a harvest, to see results. And although our salvation is none of our own doing, because of this great salvation, we now *want* to do, in gratitude to the One who has saved us.

Not too long ago, a neighbor and I discussed the finished work of Christ and how our salvation and our eternal destiny is all complete at the cross. He asked, "What then is the purpose of sanctification? What purpose does living the Christian life fulfill?"

Does fruit have a purpose? Often when people hear the words of Jesus that "without me ye can do nothing," they misunderstand and think that nothing need be done. No. Fruit is vitally important. Let's examine briefly four major reasons why fruit is important.

1. Fruit Reveals the Gardener to Others

Matthew 5:16 says, "Let your light so shine before men, that they may see your good works, and glorify your Father which is in heaven." As we bear fruit, we show the love and power of God to others, and they are drawn to Him. Bearing fruit is one of God's chosen methods for attracting others to the vineyard, to the true Vine. Do you want others to share with you in the connection you have with the Vine? Then you will be interested in bearing fruit, as a testimony to them. Fruit attracts others to the Vine.

2. Fruit Brings Glory to the Gardener and to the Vine

Psalm 23:3: "He leadeth me in the paths of righteousness for *his* name's sake." The result of our good works, our righteousness, our fruit, which He produces in our lives, is that God is glorified. And isn't the desire to glorify God a valid reason for desiring to bear fruit?

3. Fruit Comes Naturally as a Result of Connection With The Vine

Jesus says that a good tree brings forth good fruit. See Matthew 7:17. James says that a pure fountain will bring forth sweet water—not bitter. See James 3:11. Ellen White, writing in *The Desire of Ages,* page 668, tells us that when we know God as it is our privilege to know Him, sin will become hateful to us.

To the renewed heart, fruit has value in itself, because it suits the converted tastes and appetites and inclinations and desires. Fruit is attractive. It is beautiful. It is desirable. As a result of the connection with the Vine, we will not only produce fruit, but we will find fruit to be the thing we want most. This fruit is important because it fits in with our values, as branches that are connected to the true Vine.

4. We Are Saved to Bear Fruit

Sometimes we become so preoccupied with salvation itself that we forget what we are being saved from. We become like horses that are saved from a burning barn, only to run back into it the moment we are loosed. We are like prisoners released from jail who return to their cells. We are like drowning men pulled ashore only to dive back into the murky depths once more.

Never forget that salvation means you are *saved from some-*

thing. That sounds so elementary that it's almost an insult to say it. But we are not saved from sin in order to be able to go on sinning. We are saved to bear fruit, fulfilling the purpose of both our creation and redemption.

So we have in John 15, on the basis of Jesus' own teaching, the repeated hope of a harvest, the goal of fruit in the vineyard—the glory of God and the happiness of mankind.

In these verses we are reminded that it is possible to live without Him. Otherwise, why would Jesus take the pains of reminding His disciples that without Him, they could do nothing? What does it mean to be without Him? Well, it's not talking about being without Him in terms of life and health and strength. It is talking here about the close union and communion of the branch with the vine. It is possible, in other words, to live as merely a church member, to be a follower of Christ from a distance, to be in the vineyard, so to speak, without having union and communion with the Saviour. Jesus is warning against this when He says, Please, abide in Me. Stay with Me. Stay in relationship and fellowship with Me.

One of the things that makes it so easy to live without Him is our concept of what fruit is. We often deceive ourselves into thinking that we have fruit when we don't. Let's take a look at what fruit is. Let's look at the list of fruit in Galatians 5:22, 23. "The fruit of the Spirit is love, joy, peace, long-suffering, gentleness, goodness, faith, meekness, temperance: against such there is no law." Notice that all the qualities listed are inward qualities, inward attitudes. It's not talking so much about behavior and deeds and actions. It's talking about the inward graces of the heart.

Fruit is not primarily an external thing. In the earlier verses of Galatians 5, the works of the flesh are described, and there the reverse is true—they are mostly external transgressions, although there are one or two on the list, such as envy and hatred, that are qualities of the inward life.

The fruits of the Spirit are not limited to outward performance, but to the inward motives and feelings and attitudes. If we don't have that straight, then we will deceive ourselves into thinking that we have the fruit if we are performing good deeds. If the strong person can produce good deeds externally, then he fools himself into thinking that he is abiding in the vine, when he may not be at all.

When you talk about the fruits of righteousness, you are talking about the fruits of Jesus, because the greatest single definition for righteousness is Jesus. *We* have no righteousness, and as soon as you talk about righteousness, you have to be talking about Jesus, the only One in this world who was ever unblemished by sin in His life.

No wonder then that Jesus in the parable links the branches with the vine so closely and says, "Without me ye can do nothing." Fruits are never produced by the person. They are never produced by working on fruit. They are the fruit of the Spirit, and they come spontaneously as a result of being connected to the Vine.

Love is a fruit of the Spirit, never the fruit of the person. The only place to obtain love is from the Lord Jesus Himself. Peace is a fruit of the Spirit. You never find peace by summit conferences and peace talks—not real, lasting peace. It's one thing for Israel and Egypt to stop fighting each other because they are worn out and have no more fighting resources left and neither of them can survive another war. It's another thing to say they really love each other.

Joy has to be spontaneous—it isn't something you can try hard to experience. It is only Jesus who can produce any of the fruits of the Spirit—love, joy, peace, long-suffering, and all the rest. Isn't it good news to know that it is the privilege of the Christian who is living close to the true Vine to have the fruits of the Spirit naturally and spontaneously? This good news is good news today—in the twentieth century.

A third point we could notice from this Scripture is that when we do not abide in Christ, even though we might be disciples, or even prophets, like Balaam, we will end up in total failure. Zero yield.

Perhaps we still be forgiven if we spend a little bit of time on the church. When I talk about the church, I'm not talking primarily about church leadership. It is the individual who makes up the body of Christ. You are the church. I am the church. It is possible for the church today, just as Jesus indicated it was possible for the early church, to end up in total failure. A church might be able to produce certain statistical gains, great architecture, or intellectual discussion. But there are some giant cathedrals in the world that are empty, and unless Jesus Christ is the central focus of the church, it will come to total failure. That's one of the reasons why we are still here.

What is Christianity without Jesus? Nothing but a club or some kind of fraternity. We may believe that the life of Jesus is beautiful and that His example and His ethics are above reproach. But what about the central focus being Jesus? What about having Jesus as supreme, so that wherever you turn among Christian people, it's Jesus, Jesus, Jesus.

Christianity without Jesus is like bread without flour. Today people are making bread without a lot of things—without sugar, without oil, or without salt. But it's pretty hard to make bread without flour! When it comes to the Christian faith, if Jesus is not uplifted, we've missed it completely. But too many times we have missed it, too many times we have forgotten Him, and the only alternative is to end up in total failure.

Christians can get together for conferences and retreats and conventions. We have learned how to mouth the right words. The total failure becomes obvious in our doing. "Without me ye can *do* nothing." Without Him, without union and communion with Him, we may talk a lot and we may plan a lot and we may discuss a lot, but when it comes to doing anything in terms of producing fruit—nothing.

Which brings us to our fourth major point: We must come to the place where we admit that without Him we can do nothing and submit to the vine. This is where the cross comes very much into focus. When we stop doing certain things, we often talk about surrender and giving up. But surrender has more to do with giving up on ourselves than it has to do with giving up certain things. Romans 9 gives a tragic picture of God's people. Verse 31 says Israel was trying to produce fruit, and it didn't. But you have, in verse 30, a group of people who weren't trying to produce fruit, and it did. How can you explain this? Because the one group did not seek to produce fruit by faith, or by connection with the vine, but by their own efforts. Romans 10:3 says that they, being ignorant of God's way of producing fruit and going about to produce their own fruit, have not submitted them*selves* unto the fruit that comes from God, or of the Vine. For everyone who will get in touch with the grapevine, Christ is the end of trying to produce grapes apart from the grapevine. (That's Venden's Revised Paraphrased Version!)

Christ is the end of trying to produce fruit apart from the vine. When we see our condition, see our total failure to produce fruit apart from Him, even though we can run a good program in the church, even though we can keep the attention of the kiddies in the children's meetings, even though we can make it financially and be of service in the community, if we do any of it apart from the personal relationship and union with Jesus, it's total failure, regardless of what goes down on the reports.

The church as a whole and we as individual members must come to the place of admitting failure and give up on trying to produce our own fruit. We need to go to our knees like Paul and admit that the good which we try to perform, we find not. Not until this takes place can we discover what it means to be truly connected with the Vine.

When Paul said in Romans 7:18, "How to perform that which is good I find not," he was not talking about external works. In Philippians 3, he lists pretty good success on externals. He did not obviously come short there. But Paul had caught a glimpse of the real fruit, the internal fruit. As a result he went to his knees and said, I am admitting total failure apart from Jesus; I cannot produce—I cannot perform. So let's find ourselves with him there, surrendering to Jesus in the vineyard, admitting our need, and crying out for the grace that comes from above.

There is a final glimpse here that is encouraging. If without Christ His followers can do nothing, then without Christ His foes and His opponents can do less than nothing! Without Christ, those who are against the Christian faith, those who are against God's remnant church, can accomplish less than nothing. That's good news too.

There was a lunatic who stood up in a church years ago. He ranted and raved down the aisle. He shouted at the preacher, he foamed at the mouth, he said he was going to tear the church down. And he went for the pillar to pull the church down, like Samson of old.

The people began to panic, until one man spoke out calmly and said, "Let him try. Let him try."

And suddenly everybody sat down again. The cause of God goes forward in spite of what may be done to prevent it. The cause of God is going onward, and wouldn't you love to go onward with it? Without Him we can do nothing, but with Him, all things are possible.

*"Every branch in me
that beareth not fruit he taketh
away: and every branch that beareth
fruit, he purgeth it, that it may
bring forth more fruit." "If a man
abide not in me, he is cast forth
as a branch, and is withered; and
men gather them, and cast them into
the fire, and they are burned." John
15:2, 6.*

The Pruning Knife

The pruning knife of God is going to either cut you down, or cut you off—one of the two. This sounds like a rather hard-hitting topic—the pruning knife. There are some people who want to believe that all trials and troubles and hard things in life come from the devil, and it's true that many of them come from that source. But here is Bible evidence for the discipline from God Himself, as part of the process necessary to our growth and fruit bearing. I trust we will find even here words of hope and comfort, because these words were not meant to bring despair. These words of Jesus are the words of a dying Man, and not only a dying Man, but a dying Saviour. Often a man saves his best for the last. Here in John 15, just before Gethsemane and the cross, Jesus was giving some of His best.

Now one of the things we want to notice here is that God is interested in fruit. For those who are bringing forth fruit, He is interested in more fruit. And those who do not produce fruit are cut off. It's just that simple.

Verse 8 reminds us of one of the purposes of fruit bearing. "Herein is my Father glorified, that ye bear much fruit." We have already noticed that one of the purposes of fruit bearing is to bring glory to God. But let's be careful at this point that we don't get the impression that one of the purposes of fruit bearing is to save us in heaven. The fruit bearing glorifies God and enlarges His kingdom. It brings joy to us, for it fits with our natural impulses when we are abiding in the Vine, and it restores us to the original condition of mankind—that which God designed to be in the first place. But the fruit bearing is not what saves us—we are saved by accepting what Jesus has already done for us at the cross.

Yet God is interested in fruit. He is interested in character development. He is interested in seeing us saved from the results of sin and the condition of sin, as well as saving us from the penalty of sin. That's the position that this chapter in John 15 obviously takes.

In verse 2 we are faced again with this remarkable fact—that there are two types of branches, both called "in Christ," or in the vine. One bears fruit; the other doesn't bear fruit. As we have noticed earlier, it is possible to be in Christ, at least for a time, but not to bear fruit to His glory. It is possible to actually be converted, to begin the Christian life, to join the church—but if a person does not continue the abiding relationship or continue fellowship with the Lord Jesus, the fruit does not result. It is possible to make a good start, a good beginning, like Demas and others, but having loved this present life, to allow the attraction of other things to sidetrack us from our personal relationship with God.

It's the same kind of person who is described in Matthew 13, in the parable of the sower and the seed and the soil. Thorny ground. The seed is good, and the seed takes root and springs up. But the thorns interfere and choke the plants before they bear fruit.

The branches that bear no fruit represent those who fail to remain in the abiding relationship with Christ. So you have two types, one who begins, but who does not stay with Christ; and one who begins, but who does stay with Christ. Both of them are labeled "in me," in this verse. Apparently God allows those who make a good beginning, but who do not stay with Him, a period of time to demonstrate whether or not the fruit is going to be forthcoming.

We do the same thing in our gardens at home. I transplanted a tree into my yard from further down in the woods. It didn't do very well, but I left it there, not doing very well, for a long time. I wanted to be sure it was good and dead before I pulled it out. Finally I pulled it out when it proved beyond a shadow of a doubt that it was not going to bear anything, not even leaves. We know that there comes a time when branches or plants or trees have had opportunity to demonstrate themselves, and it is pointless to leave them in the garden any longer after that time.

I suppose we could speculate on just what percentage of people who make a good start are in this category. Studies have shown that the majority of church members are too busy to take even five minutes a day for personal fellowship with Christ, for private prayer and study of the Scriptures. Some surveys indicate only one in four, or one in five have any regular time for communion with God on a daily basis. This certainly is one of the reasons for the real spiritual trouble that the church finds itself in today.

Perhaps it would help to consider a little parable. Two medical students go off to school to study for medicine. One of the first things they are introduced to is the anatomy lab. In this lab there is a heavy silence. It's kind of cold, and things are really dead there!

But these medical students are anxious to make a good showing, and so they analyze the situation. They notice that there is a good deal of unity there in the lab. There don't seem to be any fights going on; no one is vying for the highest place. They're all in the same position. As the medical students consider the situation, they become convinced that what these patients need is to grow. After futile attempts to get them to grow and even trying to get them to exercise, they decide that there is an even deeper problem.

One day they wonder if the problem of these people in the lab is that they don't have any fellowship. But that turns out to be a dead-end street, for the patients there refuse to be sociable.

They even try to develop a statement of mission for "Cadaver" and his friends, but it is ignored.

In the end, the medical students discover to their dismay that all of the people in the lab have a common problem. They're not breathing. And another problem that came even earlier was that they're not eating, either.

Breathing, in the spiritual life, has been likened to prayer, the breath of the soul. And eating has been likened to the study of God's Word. If the majority of church members are not breathing or eating, it is pointless to talk of church growth.

The medical professor finally convinces these two students to examine these people in the lab to find out what caused their condition. Then they can help keep their relatives and friends from developing and degenerating into the same state.

But there is an encouraging word from Ezekiel in this analogy, when he asked, Can these dead bones live? See Ezekiel 37:3. Even among those who are in the vine, but who are not growing and not producing fruit, there is still hope that they will understand. God has never held people accountable for that which they have not understood, and that's one of the evidences of His love. God holds us responsible for that which we have had a chance to understand, and perhaps this might even include the understanding of the importance of eating and breathing.

It is possible for people to make a right start, to have a genuine conversion, and still gradually wither away because they haven't realized the necessity of abiding. It is interesting that even brilliant people for long periods of time can miss the basis of what it means to abide in Christ. But God understands the problems we face in this world of sin, and He can remove the veil that is so often over our eyes.

We are suggesting that, contrary to nature, it is possible for a large number yet to catch a vision of Jesus and the cross and become fruit bearers. That's why some of us have felt a call to evangelism of the church pew. There is a great field for evangelism within the church.

A person who is not abiding in Christ, even though he might have made a good start, will react one of two ways to the pruning knife. For one who is not aware of the love of Jesus, the pruning knife may appear to be a punishment instead of a discipline. Because he is only a servant and not a friend and perhaps does not realize his sonship yet, he may not recognize the loving Father behind the chastening. But the pruning can either lead him to be more closely connected to the Vine, and thus begin to produce fruit, or it can end up in his being cut off altogether.

The problem is that the pruning is often misunderstood. It can even be misunderstood by those who have made a good start and who have also continued in the abiding relationship with Christ. Even those who are bearing fruit are going to be purged, that they may bring forth more fruit. They are pruned, not for the purpose of being cut off, but for the purpose of being cut down to size, instead of becoming high and lifted up and forgetting that they are only creatures. This cutting-down process is often painful. But for the one who is in daily fellowship with Christ, in daily recognition of the grace of God, there is the possibility of recognizing the pruning process as a discipline, rather than a punishment. There's a word that comes from *discipline*, it's *disciple*. A disciple, or follower of Christ, is one who accepts the discipline and sees that it has meaning.

Hebrews 12:11 is a very interesting commentary on that process. "Now no chastening for the present seemeth to be joyous, but grievous: nevertheless afterward it yieldeth the peaceable fruit of righteousness unto them which are exercised thereby."

With that in mind, let's take a look at the pruning knife. What is the knife? The common idea is that the knife is affliction and that God sends affliction. But does God send affliction, or does affliction come from the devil? Then if the devil sends affliction, and God uses it, does this mean that God and the devil are partners? No! God is in charge down here, regardless of what the devil may try to do.

Consider this solution: God can use anything Satan does, or doesn't do. And He often has. Therefore, Satan, who knows that, continues to bring misery to God and people regardless, for he knows that God is going to turn something into good regardless of what he does.

The question is, Do affliction and trouble and problems really cause a person to bear more fruit? Or is it possible for a person to see the pain without the purpose? Have you ever had some kind of problem or discouragement or disappointment or sorrow, and found that instead of its bringing you into a closer relationship with Christ, that instead it tended to make you look a little more over your glasses at heaven? Have you seen it happen with others? Does affliction always bring fruit, or is it possible that at times it can actually do damage to the abiding relationship?

Is affliction really the only pruning knife? If pruning is necessary for growth, what about heaven? We are going to continue to grow and develop throughout eternity. But there won't be affliction and sorrow in heaven. So apparently there are other means for pruning—but due to the world of sin in which we find ourselves and all of the trouble that the enemy brings into our lives, God simply makes use of it to His own glory.

When you get right down to it, the real pruning knife is the Word of God, not the affliction. The affliction and sorrow and disappointment is only the handle on the knife, to get us to the knife. It is interesting to notice in this chapter in John 15, the deeper meaning of the line in verse 3, "Now are ye clean through the word." Another rendering of it is, Now are ye pruned, through the Word. The Word is what prunes. Read it in Hebrews 4:12. Here it is called a sword. "The word of God is quick, and powerful, and sharper than any twoedged sword, piercing even to the dividing asunder of soul and spirit, and of joints and marrow, and is a discerner of the thoughts and intents of the heart."

Ephesians 6 describes the gospel armor, and the sword of the Spirit is the Word of God. So when trouble and affliction and sorrow come, one person gets driven to the Word of God; and the other person resists it. So one person is drawn closer to God than before the trouble came; and the other person is farther away and less inclined toward God than before.

Have you ever gone happily on your way, with all of the blessings and all of the time-consuming factors of a busy life? And then one day you found yourself flat on your back, with no place to look but up. And have you noticed that, if you're willing, this can become the handle to the knife, and you can be driven to the Word of God and to prayer? I've seen it happen again and again—with parishioners, relatives, and friends.

If you get a whiplash and have to lie in traction, if one of your disks goes out and the doctors put you flat on your back for two or three weeks and they put the weights on, you can consider the handle on the pruning knife and realize that maybe it's not all bad to slow down once in a while, for long enough to think.

The Word of God is the pruning knife, and the Word of God liveth and abideth forever. We spend time studying God's Word in both the written form and in the actual pronouncements of God throughout eternity. We will continue to grow, and so will the fruit.

Something else that is interesting in this passage is to remember that the pruning knife goes after excess wood and foliage. How easy it is for the wood to grow. How long since you've noticed the wood in your life? Even the fruit of the Spirit can, because of our carnal nature, be turned into wood. Let me give you an example of this. One of the fruits of the Spirit is genuine faith, or trust, in God. But because of the constant pull from the flesh, from our lower nature, which can be dominated by the Holy Spirit but which is still there, how easy it is for the trust in God to turn into trust in self. Have you seen genuine faith produce fruit in your own life? It happened to Elijah. He stood on Mount Carmel and called down fire from heaven. Absolute trust in God, and the results come.

Just a little while later, he prayed for rain. He prayed seven times before God could send the rain without encouraging him to trust in himself.

However, after the thrilling confrontation at Mount Carmel

and the clear answer of the Lord, first by fire and then with rain, Elijah slipped into a reliance on self. Jezebel sent a message to Elijah, threatening him with death the next day. Forgetful of God's care, Elijah forsook his duty and fled to the wilderness.

Consider the case of a new Christian or a reawakened Christian who is filled with zeal. Then, because of the carnal nature that is always struggling for expression, that zeal is turned into fanaticism. Have you ever seen it happen?

Here is another person who has tremendous joy in the Lord, one of the fruits of the Spirit. He is overwhelmed with gratitude toward God for sending Jesus and for the finished work of Christ at the cross. Then the enemy comes in and causes him to turn to pride in his own experience instead of joy in the Lord.

Have you seen agape love, the kind of love that God has, turned by the carnal nature and the devil into erotic love? I've seen it happen.

You see a person who is gentle. He has the fruit of the Spirit that led him to gentleness. But the enemy makes him into a milquetoast.

You see another one who has meekness, which turns into an excuse for not speaking boldly for God.

You see one who has the fruit of the Spirit that is called faith, and the devil tries to get him to turn it into merely positive thinking, or some other relative of presumption.

That's why the pruning knife of God is universal and never at rest. The truth of this passage is that there is no one who isn't being pruned, or cut off. If there were someone who was perfect, he would need no more pruning. This Scripture proves that no one is bearing as much fruit as he could, and so even the fruit-bearing saints must continue to feel the knife. This process is not a one-time thing. It goes on and on, perhaps throughout eternity.

But the beautiful thing about this knife, the Word of God, is that it never condemns. Jesus came not to the world to condemn the world, but that the world through Him might be saved. See

John 3:17. If a person is not abiding in Jesus and doesn't know His love, he may think that the pruning process brings condemnation. But for the one who knows God and has a loving relationship with Him, He realizes that God's love never fails.

In conclusion, it is good news that it is God that cuts off and that God does the pruning, not man. We don't do the pruning, and we don't cut off. It is God that takes away, and He knows when the time is right. We can be thankful today that we are in the hands of a God of love, who knows how to purge for our good. Won't you please join me in seeking such a relationship with Him that when the pruning times come, we will be only cut down, but not cut off.

*"Herein is my
Father glorified, that ye bear
much fruit; so shall ye be my
disciples." "Ye have not chosen
me, but I have chosen you, and
ordained you, that ye should go
and bring forth fruit, and that
your fruit should remain." John
15:8, 16.*

Genuine Fruit

One of the key words in John 15 is *fruit*. The Lord Jesus, in His great plan of redemption, is anxious for fruit. He wants much fruit. As we have seen, if there is no fruit, the branches are cut off and burned. The gospel includes more than the forgiveness of sins. It includes the removal of sin and its replacement with the graces of the Spirit.

Perhaps the closest we can come to a definition of fruit is to consider it in terms of results. When we plant a garden, we want results. If we plant a grapevine, we want results. Fruit, in its broadest sense, would be simply results.

Sometimes people ask why, if one of the major characteristics of fruit is its spontaneity, and if fruit comes as a result rather than as a cause, then why stress fruit at all? Why did Jesus have so much to say about fruit? It's another way of asking, If good works are the result of faith, then why talk much at all about good works? Why not just talk about faith? If fruit is the sure result on a healthy vine, why spend any time on the fruit? Let's just spend our time on the vine.

Yet Jesus spent time talking about fruit; and He did it on more than one occasion. Matthew 7 is a classic example of this. Here Jesus concludes His analogy by saying that people are going to be known by their fruits—"By their fruits ye shall know them." Verse 20.

We have seen that the fruits of the Spirit are inward qualities, but for people to be known by their fruits, there must be an outward manifestation as well. I could have all kinds of love on the inside, but unless it is manifest on the outside, nobody is going to know me by my fruit. I could have all kinds of joy on the inside, but sometimes people doubt this when they see how poker-faced I get up front! No one is going to know about joy on the inside unless it is somehow manifest on the outside, perhaps by a smile or by singing or by praise. In fact, true love, joy, and the other qualities of a true Christian cannot help but find outward expression if they exist inwardly.

If we follow Jesus' analogy of the vine and the branches, it is obvious that fruit is external to the branch. But it cannot be produced externally unless it is first internal. So when we speak of fruit, we are talking about both aspects, internal and external. We're talking about the inward fruit of the Spirit—love, joy, peace, long-suffering, and so forth; and we are also talking about their manifestations on the outside.

One of the reasons Jesus emphasized genuine fruit is that, as we all know, it is possible to produce the exterior form without having the interior reality. Television actors and movie producers are very much aware that it is possible to produce a smile on call, to have in the script, "smile here." Some people can produce a most genuine-appearing smile or cry real tears simply by turning some inner switch. It is possible to have "works" without faith.

It is possible for strong-willed people to refrain from producing *bad* fruit, and, in so doing, fool themselves into thinking that they are secure. They forget that Jesus cursed the fig tree, not because it produced bad fruit, but because it didn't produce *any* fruit. The issue in the vine and the branches and the grapes is not whether we are producing bad fruit. The real issue is whether the genuine fruit of the Spirit is present, with both inward and outward manifestations.

So when we think of the fruit of the Spirit, as listed in Galatians 5, "love, joy, peace, longsuffering, gentleness, goodness,

faith, meekness, temperance," then let's also consider that ulti-
mately these fruits must be externally expressed. James points
out that it is not enough for a Christian to wish a poor, starving
person well. He must feed and clothe him to show true love. Joy
will be manifest in praise and singing. True inward peace enabled Daniel to remain calm in the lions' den. Peace will be
manifest in people who are able to sleep at night, without toss-
ing and turning and taking tranquilizers and all the rest of it.
The inward fruits will have external results.

Another reason for examining the fruit and studying it, is so
as not to miss the great lesson of Jesus' parable, that fruit
comes naturally and spontaneously. I'd like to remind you once
more that if we choose to abide in Jesus, if we choose the genuine relationship with Him, the fruit is going to be coming. If I
don't want any genuine fruit in my life, I have to move my
choice way back to the point of choosing whether or not to abide
in Christ. If I choose to continue an abiding relationship with
Jesus, I am choosing at the same time to bear fruit. I don't
choose to have an abiding relationship with Jesus and then
choose whether or not to have fruit in addition to that. I have
already chosen to produce fruit if I choose to abide in Him. The
fruit is going to be there.

Let's look at the reverse now. The only way I am *not* going to
have fruit is to choose not to have a relationship with Jesus.
The only way I'm not going to have any grapes in the vineyard
is to choose not to have any vines or branches in my vineyard. If
I have a vineyard and choose to plant vines that have branches,
I have already chosen to have grapes. I don't choose the grapes
separately; they are part of the package.

Fruit is as natural as the flowers that bloom in the
springtime. I wish that everyone could share the excitement of
this insight into the life of the Christian. Why is this exciting?
Because so many of us have wasted time and effort, again and
again, trying to produce fruit. It is a misplacement of time and
effort. It is putting the effort where it does not belong—and will
not do any good. So this becomes one of the major break-

throughs in understanding salvation by faith. It also causes a person to become a spontaneous witness, for he cannot keep quiet when he begins to find something that works, in place of something that doesn't work.

If you are abiding in Christ, in a genuine, personal, daily faith relationship, the fruit is already growing. Whether it's internal or external, the fruit is already growing.

Right here some people become rather nervous, because they don't feel as if they've seen much fruit. Well, I haven't seen much fruit on some of my plants at home. I love lilacs. We used to go out to grandmother's house, with the kerosene lamps and the old-fashioned pantry and the oilcloth tablecloth and the woodstove and the lilac bushes outside, heavily laden with lilacs every spring. They looked good; they smelled good. And things that bring delight and joy to you when you are small are not soon forgotten. So I planted a lilac bush at our place last year. I haven't seen any lilacs yet. There are branches and lilac leaves, but no blossoms.

But if that little wisp of a plant is abiding in the ground, where its roots and tendrils are becoming more and more enmeshed in the soil, then the lilacs are on their way, even though we can't see them yet. Somewhere, hidden in those stems and leaves, they are there. One of these days I am going to be overjoyed to see the lilacs. But in the meantime, I take courage because I see the leaves.

It's a very important sequence, both in the natural and the spiritual sense, that the external fruit always follows the internal fruit. It's never the other way around, where genuine growth is taking place. As Jesus described, it's "first the blade, then the ear, *after that* the full corn in the ear." Mark 4:28, emphasis supplied. How often we wish we could start with the outside, get it patched up, and then finish off the job by working on the inside. But it never happens. Fruit is never the cause; it is ever and always the result.

The only genuine obedience there is comes as a result of this abiding connection with the Vine. The plants and flowers do not grow by their own care or anxiety or effort. No more can we secure spiritual growth by such means. The plants and flowers grow by accepting the gifts of sunshine and water and nourishment that are given to them from their surroundings. So it is with the Christian life and growth. Abiding in Him, we receive the gifts He has intended, which bring growth and fruitfulness.

The Saviour does not bid His disciples labor to bear fruit; He bids them to abide in Him—See *The Desire of Ages,* p. 677. The fruit that comes is the result of a loving relationship and is natural and spontaneous. That characteristic is one of the greatest proofs that it is genuine fruit.

*"These things have
I spoken unto you, that my joy
might remain in you, and that
your joy might be full." John 15:11.*

The Fruit Is a Gift

Suppose I came to you and offered to give you $10 million. Would you accept it willingly, gladly, instantly? Or would you have trouble with the offer? Probably your first reaction would be, What's the catch?

I can still remember the time a preacher offered a dollar to a group of high-school students. He said, "I have a dollar that I want to give to someone." Most everyone said, "Ha ha." And they just sat there.

But my brother jumped to his feet, walked down, and collected the dollar. I was upset by that little move, since it was my brother! I found out later that he had already heard about this maneuver on the part of this preacher and was ready for him! But no one moved except the one who had heard about it.

You multiply that dollar by ten million, and you could have real difficulty in trying to accept that as a gift. We are used to earning what we get. I receive a paycheck from the conference that I work for. I have never yet made a trip down to the office to thank them for that check! We earn those checks we receive from our employers! True thankfulness and genuine thanksgiving come when we receive something that we have done nothing to earn or merit. That's when we really say thanks—*if* we are able to accept the gift!

Perhaps that's part of what the psalmist meant by the *sacri-*

fice of thanksgiving. See Psalm 107:22. To give thanks is to admit that you have not earned or merited the gift and that can be a real sacrifice to the proud heart.

In John 15:11 Jesus speaks of the joy that comes as a result of abiding in the vine and of finding genuine fruit manifest in the life. Notice whose joy it is: "These things have I spoken unto you, that *my* joy might remain in you, and that your joy might be full." Emphasis supplied. The disciples were to be filled with joy and thanksgiving—but even the joy came from the Vine, not from within themselves. It all is a gift, received through connection with the Vine.

When we boast about a gift, it is usually because we feel that we have somehow earned it. We say, "So-and-so appreciated my help, so they gave me this fancy present. Isn't it lovely?" We thereby honor the gift—and ourselves. But how often have you heard someone say something like this? "So-and-so gave me this fancy present because they are so loving and generous and kind. I've done absolutely nothing for them, but now they've given me this present, in spite of the fact that I have hurt and abused them again and again. They must have given me this present because they are so filled with love that somehow they love me. Aren't they wonderful?" Is there a difference between the two? Watch yourself getting mixed up in the gifts that you think you have accepted for free!

Genuine thanksgiving has to be voluntary. Genuine thanksgiving has to be prompted by love, not duty. And genuine thanksgiving accepts not only the gift, but the giver as well, because you cannot separate the gift from the giver. There are people who want to accept the gift of salvation, and the goodies that come with it, without accepting the Giver. But that's impossible.

Remember Cain and Abel? Both Cain and Abel had been given the same instructions. But Cain offered fruit *instead* of the sacrifice of thanksgiving. He brought that which was interlaced with his own labors, and therefore his sacrifice was unacceptable. He wasn't really thankful for what God had done for him; he wanted to have part of the credit. He hadn't accepted the message of John 15, the message of this vineyard parable, that he could do nothing without God, but that through connection with the Giver, he could receive freely the fruits provided.

Abel followed the instructions that God had given, which was to bring a sacrifice. The sacrifice was a symbol that there was nothing he could do. The Lamb represented the One who was to come and do it all.

To try to force the fruit in the Christian life is to destroy the fruit. If we see Christ on the cross and say, "He died for me; I must pay Him back by trying to force myself to bear fruit," we are not accepting His gift at all. It is impossible to pay for the "unspeakable gift." See 2 Corinthians 9:15. When we see Him on the cross and respond to Him in love because of His kindness and mercy to us, we will not be too proud to also accept the gift of fruit to His glory that He wants to give us—and, through us, to the world.

The problem is that there are many people who do not want to accept a gift they cannot pay back. As a result, they follow this pattern: They say, "If I can't pay you back for what you gave me, I want nothing to do with you at all." Have you seen it happen in your own life? When we genuinely want to give something and someone insists on paying for it, this sort of takes the joy out of giving. Have you ever had it happen?

Thousands of people are making this mistake in terms of salvation. They refuse to accept Christ's gift unless they can do something to pay Him back. The truth is that all we can ever produce in an attempt to pay Him back is unacceptable.

When we realize the enormity of His gift and the depth of His love and unite ourselves to Him through faith day by day, the fruit of that experience will be seen in our lives. His love will be manifest in us, His joy will fill our hearts, His peace will keep our hearts and minds. We will offer true thanksgiving to Him for His unspeakable gift.

"If ye abide in me,
and my words abide in you, ye
shall ask what ye will, and it
shall be done unto you."
"Whatsoever ye shall ask of the
Father in my name, he may give it
you." John 15:7, 16.

Asking What You Will

There has been a great deal of misunderstanding on prayer in the Christian religion. Some of us have searched for the complete book on prayer and have yet to find it. There are many good books on the subject, and you can find one good point here and another there; but there seems to be not a single book that sums it all up. We are way overdue for a greater understanding of this vital subject.

This study of the vineyard parable leads us directly into the subject of prayer, and it's interesting that Jesus included the subject in this crucial discourse. Let's read again Christ's words from John 15:7, 16: "If ye abide in me, and my words abide in you, ye shall ask what ye will, and it shall be done unto you." "Ye have not chosen me, but I have chosen you, and ordained you, that ye should go and bring forth fruit, and that your fruit should remain: that whatsoever ye shall ask of the Father in my name, he may give it you."

This two-verse duo give what appears to be a blank check. All you have to do is fill in the details, and so long as you use the words, "In Jesus' name," it will happen. This has long been the concept that many people have of prayer. Let's look at it a little closer.

First of all, we can take courage in the fact that the person who is abiding in Christ is going to ask. It doesn't say, If you abide in me, and my words abide in you, you *can* ask, or you *may* ask, or you *might* ask. It says, you *shall* ask.

I understand the scientific conclusion is unanimous that people who are alive breathe. For people who are alive, breathing is a rather natural process. Even brand-new babies breathe. Prayer has been likened to the breath of the soul, and there is going to be a lot of spontaneous praying on the part of the Christian.

There is also a deliberate taking time for prayer that is a part of the abiding spoken of in John 15. But one of the results of abiding in Christ is prayer, the spontaneous prayer life that includes talking to God as to a friend. Could it be that both deliberate and spontaneous prayer are indicated here in these verses?

John 15:7 says, "It shall be done unto you." Some of us have had the idea that we somehow had to answer our own prayers. But the promise is that if we ask, it shall be done unto us. This immediately reminds us that God is in control, God is in charge, and the one who is abiding in Christ will be controlled by the Spirit of God. It isn't so much what I am doing; it's what He is doing through me. This explains the phrase, "It shall be done unto you." It suggests our being simply instruments. It suggests the idea of total abandonment, the idea of surrender and total relinquishment. It does away with the idea that we do part, and God does part. If we abide in Him, He's going to do it unto us. Are you willing, or does that scare you? Are we willing for that sort of total abandonment and surrender?

Another thing we notice in this text is that the cart blanche is for "abiders." It is for those who are abiding, and let's not miss that. What's going to happen if the person who is not abiding in Christ asks whatever he wants? He will ask for something that is not included in the promise.

The one who is abiding in Christ has already given over the control to Christ, not only of the externals, but of the internals as well. When Christ comes in and takes control, He changes the heart. He changes the springs of action in our mind: the desires, the tastes, the inclinations. It is easy to read a text like Psalm 37:4—"Delight thyself also in the Lord; and he shall give thee the desires of thine heart—" and say, "Oh good! Anything I want, I get." But there's another way to read it: "*He* shall give thee the *desires*" plural. If His words are abiding in us and we are abiding in Him, if we have surrendered to Him our will, then to ask what *we* will is the same as asking for what *He* wills.

Now I would like to examine with you a sort of two-pronged methodology for answered prayer. It says, "If you abide in Me, *and* My words abide in you." These become the two feet by which we climb to the mountaintop of power in prayer.

The first, "If you abide in Me," suggests that a beginning has already been made; that's why He can ask us to stay with Him. We could not abide in Him if we had never yet come to Him. This also reminds us that the beginning and the continuation is the same insofar as method is concerned. How did you first become a Christian? By accepting totally what Jesus had done for you; by giving up on self and simply casting yourself at the feet of Jesus, admitting that He had to be a total and complete Saviour; by resting your hope of eternal life on nothing else than Jesus Christ. To abide in Him is to stay in that stance, to continue to base our hope of eternal life totally and solely upon what Jesus has done, and to base none of our hope on what we ourselves can do.

Now it's one thing to accept that premise when we first come to Jesus, and it can be quite another thing to stay with that premise in the continuing Christian life. Remember what Jesus said, "If ye continue in my word, then are ye my disciples indeed." John 8:31. It's one thing to be a disciple to begin with; it is another thing to continue to be a disciple of Jesus by continuing in His Word.

We've also noticed that God has methods of purging the branches, pruning branches that are in the Vine, and it is sometimes one thing to abide in Him at the beginning of the purging and pruning, and another to remain abiding in Him at the end of the process. I would like to remain in Him as much after the fiery trial as before the fiery trial, wouldn't you? So abiding in Him is one of the feet by which we climb to the mountain of success in prayer.

Notice Elijah again. When he was on top of Mount Carmel and prayed for fire to come down from heaven, it came. Just like that. But when he asked for rain, it didn't happen at first. Elijah's prayer for rain was not answered until he had prayed a number of times. So it is possible to be purged by success, rather than simply through trial and adversity.

The devil is happy if he can cause us to become discouraged over our failures. He's equally happy when he can cause us to be separated from God because of our successes. Many of us can't stand much fruit. We begin taking the glory to ourselves.

The second of these two feet by which we climb to power in prayer is, "If My words abide in you." Sometimes people have seen a difference of thought between Jesus and His Word. The truth is that Jesus *is* the Word. John 1 is very clear on that. There is no separation. The person who comes along and says, "Well, I believe in the Lord Jesus, and I am relying totally on Him; but what His Word has to say in terms of certain doctrines and teachings is quite another thing"—that person is making one of the greatest of errors. There is no such separation possible. Therefore, the person who thinks he is abiding in Christ, but who does not have His words abiding in him as well, is not really qualified for the blank check of this promise, "Ye shall ask what ye will, and it shall be done unto you." There are two conditions, let's face it. There is a big IF—"If My words abide in you." To accept Jesus is to accept His Word; to not accept His Word is to not accept Jesus. And of course, that's one of the things about truth—it is a progression, a constant growth, like a light "that shineth more and more unto the perfect day." See Proverbs 4:18.

Now I'd like to ask the question, Why is it that these conditions must be met in order for the blank check to be honored? Why must this tremendous blessing that is promised, "Whatsoever ye ask in My name, I will do it," be contingent upon abiding in Him? Why must it only be received in this way?

Well, in the first place, it is because the branch, if it is connected to the Vine, is going to be receiving only what the Vine has to give. The sap and the continual growth of the two together, in connection and deeper connection, simply suggests a oneness that keeps a person from asking wrongly that he may consume it upon his own lusts.

What would happen, for instance, if God were to go to the man on the street, who cares nothing for God or faith or religion or the Bible, and give him this blank check: "Look, you can ask whatever you want, and I'll do it"? Perhaps the man on the street would ask for another drink. Perhaps he would ask for permission and freedom and opportunity to enjoy his own lusts. Perhaps he would ask for riches or success that would drive him even farther from realizing his need of God. God is not in the business of encouraging this kind of thing.

Let's suppose that God were to make this offer to the nominal Christian, one who does not place much value on association with Jesus. A person who is living apart from Christ is hopelessly self-centered; he was born that way, and his requests would inevitably be selfish requests. I'd like to suggest to you that the professed Christian who does not know a close connection with Jesus is one of the most self-centered people in the world. You might even have people out in the world who are more gracious and courteous and kind, than a professed Christian who lives a life apart from Jesus. So if God were to give this blank check to one who was not abiding in Him, there would be the potential of all kinds of self-centered requests—and the book of James comes down on that rather hard.

Another reason why we can receive only in this way is that God intends us to meet Him with His own words. If we abide in Him, and His words abide in us—that means we are familiar with His words. We know what He has said on a given subject. Have you ever been hit with your own words? I've had it happen again and again, particularly with my children. Perhaps I had forgotten what I had said concerning what we were going to do or where we were going to go or what we were going to get. And I've had my children say to me, "But Daddy, you *said* . . ."

I know I'm finished right there! The story is over. I have been hit with my own words. When I suddenly remember those words, I know that there is no point in trying to discuss it any longer.

If we are the children of God, the sons and daughters of God, and we come to God with His own words, do we not find them in a similar category? Someone has called it "overcoming omnipotence with omnipotence."

Let's go to a few of God's own words. The first is recorded in Matthew 7:7-11. It is a well-known passage. We won't go all the way through it; you know the words. Ask, seek, knock. And then verse 11: "If ye then, being evil, know how to give good gifts unto your children, how much more shall your Father which is in heaven give good things to them that ask him?"

In Matthew, this particular passage closes right here. But we find a parallel passage in Luke 11, and that's the one we will look at more closely. "And he said unto them, Which of you shall have a friend, and shall go unto him at midnight, and say unto him, Friend, lend me three loaves; for a friend of mine in his journey is come to me, and I have nothing to set before him? And he from within shall answer and say, Trouble me not: the door is now shut, and my children are with me in bed; I cannot rise and give thee. I say unto you, Though he will not rise and give him, because he is his friend, yet because of his importunity he will rise and give him as many as he needeth.

"And I say unto you, Ask, and it shall be given you; seek, and ye shall find; knock, and it shall be opened unto you. For every one that asketh receiveth; and he that seeketh findeth; and to him that knocketh, it shall be opened. If a son shall ask bread of any of you that is a father, will he give him a stone? or if he ask a fish, will he for a fish give him a serpent? Or if he shall ask an egg, will he offer him a scorpion? If ye then, being evil, know how to give good gifts unto your children: how much more shall your heavenly Father give the Holy Spirit to them that ask him?" Luke 11:5-13.

What is the context? It is that if a person comes to God, asking God for something to help another, he can know that his request is going to be heard and answered, like a father to a son. The qualification is that He will give the Holy Spirit—and how much higher is that than a new Cadillac or a new house or a new Honda?

Would it be safe to conclude, then, that this passage is speaking of asking in service, in the framework of working for others?

Now let's go to John 14:12, 13 for further insight. "Verily, verily, I say unto you, He that believeth on me, the works that I do shall he do also, and greater works than these shall he do." What kind of works did Jesus do? For what purpose were His life, His work, His miracles, and His teachings? For others—for reaching out for the sake of the gospel of the kingdom. Then comes the next verse, with the promise, "Whatsoever ye shall ask in my name, that will I do, that the Father may be glorified in the Son." What's the context again? It is the context of service and outreach for the sake of the gospel.

What a travesty upon the honor of the Word of God to take a text like that out of context and apply it to something we want or desire for ourselves.

Matthew 21:22 gives a clue in understanding this: "All things, whatsoever ye shall ask in prayer, believing, ye shall receive." Its parallel passage, found in Mark 11:20-24 tells the story of the cursed fig tree, and the mountain, and carries with it the qualification, that we must have the faith to truly believe in God's power.

Is there anyone with a tree in his yard he wants moved? Does anyone have a mountain he'd like to have put somewhere else? What about poison oak? I've got some poison oak I'd like to get rid of. Could I go out tomorrow morning in the name of Jesus and curse my poison oak and hug this text to my chest? Would I be able to approach such a project without doubting? Or should this passage also be understood as having to do with service for others and the advancing of the work of Christ?

There's another factor to consider with this verse about not doubting. Sometimes with our short line of human vision, we ask for things that are not God's will. What do we do when our requests are denied? Do we walk away in anger from a God who has disappointed our expectations? Or do we do as did Job, and in the face of whatever sorrow or disappointment continue to love and trust Him regardless. Do we have faith and doubt *Him* not?

Another similar text is found in 1 John 3:21-24: "Beloved, if our heart condemn us not, then have we confidence toward God. And whatsoever we ask, we receive of him, because we keep his commandments, and do those things that are pleasing in his sight. And this is his commandment, That we should believe on the name of his Son Jesus Christ, and love one another, as he gave us commandment. And he that keepeth his commandments dwelleth in him, and he in him."

So, on the basis of God's Word, if we have some known sin or continuation in transgression in our lives, then we'd better not expect the carte blanche that He has offered. This is also suggested in Isaiah 59:1, 2.

Then back to our original chapter, we read in John 15:16, "I have chosen you, and ordained you." Jesus ordained His disciples for what purpose? To go out and spread the gospel of the kingdom. He ordained them for service, to do the same kind of work that He did, that they should go and bring forth fruit. Then comes the phrase again, "Whatsoever ye shall ask of the Father in my name, he may give it you." The context again is obviously service. So it would be safe to suggest that as we approach these promises—that whatever we ask in Jesus' name, He is going to do—that we approach them in the setting in which they were given.

The entire setting of John 15 has to do with abiding and fruit bearing for the glory of God.

Jesus has made it possible for us to dwell in Him, and for Him to dwell in us, so that His will and our will are swallowed up together as one will. He has made it possible for His desires and our desires to be one and the same. Now let me ask you this question: If my heart is united to His heart, if my will is submerged in His will, and if my mind becomes one with His mind, would it be safe for Him to respond to anything that I might ask Him in the name of Jesus? In a sense, it's as if Jesus were saying to me, "If you want exactly what I want, you can ask whatever you want, and I'll do it!"

These words in John 15 are addressed to mature Christians. But, you may ask, who qualifies? I would like to remind you of the good news that when the branch abides in the vine, that the branch is just as valuable to the Gardener as is the vine. Jesus said, "I am the vine, ye are the branches." God loves us as He loves Jesus. As we continue to abide in Him, we know that the carte blanche He has in mind for us is potential, *so long as*. We will look more closely at the "so long as" factor in the next chapter. But this promise can be realized *so long as* we abide in the vine. It's not reserved for down somewhere toward the end of our lives.

On that basis, I am going to predict that there are times when, like Elijah, you have seen the fire come down from heaven; and there are times when, like Elijah, you have felt that your prayers are unanswered. Elijah didn't have to wait until just before he was translated to get the blank check. He had the blank check when he was trusting, and he did not have it when he was not trusting. The same is true for you and me.

In the meantime, Jesus loves you, and God loves you just as much as He loves the vine. He will continue to prune and purge you for His purposes and His glory.

"Abide in me, and I in you. As the branch cannot bear fruit of itself, except it abide in the vine; no more can ye, except ye abide in me." John 15:4.

Two Kinds of Abiding

Several years ago I was waiting to board an airplane in Los Angeles. The fog was thick, and out there somewhere in the fog was the plane we were supposed to take to Chicago. It sounded something like this: "rrrrrRRRRRR—cough! cough!" And every time that engine would cough and choke and spit, a few more passengers would fade away into the darkness, until, when we finally left at around 2:00 a.m., I was about the only passenger on board! I had a hard time letting my weight down all the way to Chicago.

Have you ever experienced living a Christian life that sounded like that airplane? Have you ever wondered if your flight of Christian life was ever going to get off the ground? Have you ever experienced coming to Christ, seeking to abide in Him, but then realized your weakness and despaired of ever producing fruit?

Inherent in this vineyard parable of Jesus are two kinds of abiding, and it can be very important to understand the distinction between them.

The first we might call the abiding *relationship;* the second, the abiding *dependence.*

Let's go back to the grapevine in an attempt to understand the difference between these two phases of abiding in the vine. When a branch is grafted onto the vine, a relationship is begun, an association is begun. The branch and the vine are together, and so long as they *stay* together, the second phase of abiding can begin to take place.

The second kind of abiding is the moment by moment dependence of the branch upon the vine. Because of the association begun at the time of grafting, a deeper abiding begins. The sap from the vine begins flowing through to the branch. The little fibers and tendrils become enmeshed, until, little by little, the two are as one. This second kind of connection does not happen overnight. It involves a process of growth. It is always dependent upon the abiding *relationship* continuing. If the branch is severed from the vine, all process of union between the cells and fibers of the branch and vine is immediately cut off, and no further growth can take place until the abiding *relationship* is once again established. The abiding *dependence* develops over a period of time, not instantaneously, and it is able to happen only when the branch is connected to the vine in the abiding *relationship*.

When we come to Christ and begin a day-by-day personal relationship with Him, and keep on coming, we have established an abiding *relationship*. This relationship continues as long as we continue coming to Him day by day for fellowship and communion in His Word and through prayer.

The abiding *dependence*, or second kind of abiding, comes as a result of this abiding relationship. As we continue to seek Jesus day by day, as we learn more and more of His love for us and behold Him as He is revealed in His Word, we are led to depend upon Him moment by moment.

The abiding relationship is where we put our effort. We can make a deliberate choice to continue seeking fellowship with Christ. The abiding dependence is God's work—He will bring us to that experience so long as we continue the abiding relationship with Him.

When we first come to Christ, when we are first united to the Vine, He begins His work in our lives. We are accepted before God as though we had never ever even sinned. But there is more to salvation than the initial acceptance. Jesus said in Matthew 10 that those who endure to the end will be saved. See verse 22. We must not only come once, but we must keep on coming, in order for the connection between the vine and the branch to remain.

We are told in 1 John 3:6 that "whosoever abideth in him sinneth not." Have you ever experienced setting aside time each day for communion and fellowship with Christ, and yet finding that you still failed in living the victorious Christian life? The disciples experienced that. They walked with Jesus for three and a half years, and yet at the time of the parable of the vineyard, they still had not yet understood how to *depend* on Him all of the time. *Steps to Christ* gives this further amplification of 1 John 3:6: "If we abide in Christ, if the love of God dwells in us, our feelings, our thoughts, our purposes, our actions, will be in harmony with the will of God."—Page 61.

I'd like to propose that most of us have experienced times of this kind of abiding dependence, when our will and God's will were somehow merged into one. But we are also painfully aware that we do not always depend on Him in this way. That is where the danger comes in.

Sometimes the devil causes us to take our eyes off Jesus for a moment, and we fall and fail and sin. He would like us to become discouraged. He would like for us to believe that the abiding *relationship* is not working and that we might as well give it up until the next week of prayer or revival. But Ellen White, in *Steps to Christ,* page 64, reminds us, "We shall often have to bow down and weep at the feet of Jesus because of our shortcomings and mistakes, but we are not to be discouraged. Even if we are overcome by the enemy, we are not cast off, not forsaken and rejected of God."

As we have already mentioned, the abiding relationship day by day is where our effort comes in. It takes our willpower and determination and backbone to set aside that quiet time with Him. At times it will take every ounce of energy that we possess to seek God. And this is not something God can do for us.

But the moment-by-moment abiding dependence is God's work. Only God can lead us to that experience. "No man can empty himself of self. We can only consent for Christ to accomplish the work."—*Christ's Object Lessons,* p. 159. We can never crucify ourselves. We can never bring ourselves to the point of death to self and total dependence upon God. But if we continue to seek Him day by day in the abiding relationship, He will surely bring us to the abiding dependence upon Him.

The abiding relationship brings the assurance of salvation. The abiding dependence upon His power brings obedience and victory and overcoming in the Christian life. The abiding relationship is a day-by-day experience, the abiding dependence happens moment by moment. The growth in the Christian life comes as we learn more and more constantly to depend upon God's power instead of our own.

*"As the Father hath
loved me, so have I loved you:
continue ye in my love." John 15:9.*

It Takes Time

When I was a boy helping my folks with their garden, one of
the first things I can remember planting was radishes. Radishes are pretty good plants to get started—according to the
seed packets it takes something under two weeks to grow a radish! But even that was too long for me—and so I'd go out to the
garden every day or so and pull up the little radish plants to see
how they were coming along. This did not help the radishes to
mature any more rapidly!

Now I wouldn't want to insult a radish. But after you have
planted the seed, and waited the necessary time, you still have
only a radish! If you are interested in something more lasting—
like a giant redwood—then growth is measured in terms of
years, rather than in terms of days.

One of the pitfalls in the abiding relationship with Christ is
that we tend to forget that it takes *time* to grow fruit. We start
looking for instant results, and the very analogy of growing
fruit should remind us at once that there is a time factor involved. It doesn't happen overnight.

In Luke 13 Jesus told of a man who came looking for fruit on
a fig tree, and finding none, wanted to cut it down. The advice
of his gardener was to fertilize the ground around it and wait
for the next season, when it might well bear fruit. There *is* a
time for fruit, developed in its fullness. But one of the most dis-

couraging things we can do in the Christian life is to look for a perpetual harvest. We don't do that in the natural world. We don't expect perpetual harvest from our backyard gardens. If the time factor is important in the natural world, how much more important to remember it in the spiritual life as well!

How often we become impatient while waiting for the fruit to develop. How often we become impatient with just waiting, period! Human beings are not known for their patience. We are looking for the shortest line at the supermarket, the shortest line at the toll booth on the highway, the shortest line to the kingdom of heaven.

Waiting is perhaps the most intense form of the pruning and purging process that there is. Waiting shows us our true selves, our true values, our true motives. There are many things we will accept and seek if there is no wait involved. But when we find we have to wait, how often we discover that what we thought was so desirable is simply not worth waiting for.

Through the Bible history, we see people standing in line, as it were, waiting for the promised blessing of the Lord. Adam and Eve were in line as soon as they left the garden, waiting for the promised Messiah. Noah waited for 120 years for the Flood to come and vindicate his reliability as a prophet of God. Moses waited forty years on the back side of Mount Horeb, tending sheep. Then he waited through another forty years with the people of Israel, as they learned the lesson of waiting on the Lord. Finally he could stand the waiting no longer, and his faith failed just on the borders of the land of promise.

David was anointed king of Israel, but had to wait. Elijah expected an immediate revival and deliverance after the day at Mount Carmel, but had to wait. The disciples expected Jesus to set up His kingdom, but had to wait. They were told to wait for the promise of the Father, the outpouring of the Holy Spirit after Christ's ascension. The saints described in Revelation are distinguished by their patience in waiting.

There are very few facets of the Christian life that do not involve waiting in one form or another. We wait for the answer to our prayers. We wait to see the fruits developed in our lives. We wait for the promised return of Jesus, to bring all other waiting to an end.

So remember that it takes time to transform the human nature into the divine. You cannot reach the full measure of the stature of Christ in a day. We are to live one day at a time, continuing the abiding relationship with Him, and the harvest will surely come in its appointed time.

If you are concerned because you don't think you see much fruit in your own life, remember the parable of the vineyard. The results are sure, if we continue to abide in Him. But we must not forget the words of James in James 5:7, "The husbandman waiteth for the precious fruit of the earth, and hath long patience for it." Our part is to continue to abide in Him, and He will accomplish His part in His own time.

When you understand your part in the growth process and continue to seek that abiding relationship with Him, His work will go forward to produce in you the fruits to His glory. And you will be prepared to meet Him in peace on that day when we will say, "Lo, this is our God; we have *waited* for him, and he will save us: this is the Lord; we have *waited* for him, we will be glad and rejoice in his salvation." Isaiah 25:9, emphasis supplied.

"_____ ____ ____ ____ __
__ ____ ____ _____
____ ____ ___ ." *John 15:___* .

The Text That Isn't There!

Did you miss anything in our study of the process of gardening and growing of fruit? Are you conscious of a text or concept or idea that you think should have been present? There is a popular aspect of how gardening parallels the Christian life, that is strangely absent from this parable of Jesus about the vineyard.

Can you guess what it is? It's what to do about the weeds! What about pulling weeds? Aren't we supposed to help out with that project? Have you ever tried to do the job of weeding in your spiritual garden? Perhaps a closer look at the reason for the missing text will help us to understand the work of the branches and the work of the Husbandman.

Remember at the beginning of this volume we noticed that God is the Gardener. Scripture often speaks of God under that analogy. Who is it who does the weed pulling in the garden? I can tell you who had to do it in every garden I've come in contact with! It wasn't the plants themselves! They were completely helpless to pull weeds.

It is truth in the natural world that is so simple and obvious that it is almost embarrassing to mention it—but it is the Gardener who pulls the weeds! We could have included this truth under John 15:2 in the discussion of the purging process. Perhaps the pruning knife is as close to a weed puller as we will come in the parable of the vineyard. Notice who it is who does the pruning—is it the branches or the Husbandman? The answer is obvious.

But how often have we missed it in the spiritual world. It is a simple truth, but we have not understood it in our own lives. How easy it is, when confronted with the weeds and thorns and thistles, to begin tugging away at them, trying to take care of our own pruning process. All the time we are trying to do the impossible.

The next time you notice the weeds in your part of the vineyard, remember the missing text in John 15. Your work is never to attack the bad habit, the sin, or the fault of character. Your work is to continue the connection with the Vine and to submit by that means to the pruning knife of the Husbandman, who will take care of the weeds for you, so long as you continue to abide in Him.